Slow
COOKER
SOUPS

ISBN-13: 978-1-56383-490-5
Item #7136

**Printed in the USA
by G&R Publishing Co.**

Distributed By:

CQ Products

507 Industrial Street
Waverly, IA 50677

www.cqbookstore.com

gifts@cqbookstore.com

CQ Products

CQ Products

@cqproducts

@cqproducts

Ah, the Slow Cooker...

that magical caldron, perfect for simmering soups, bringing out the best of all the flavors you can cram into it. And if it's flavor you're after *(and of course you are)*, follow these tips for the best.

- **On a budget?** Inexpensive meats become tender and juicy morsels when slow-cooked, so don't be afraid to use them.

- **Raw meat or cooked?** Browning before slow-cooking adds nice color and a hint of caramalized yumminess *(drain off grease before adding to cooker)*, but raw can be used, too – just make sure the meat is done before serving.

- **Alcohol as part of your cooking liquid?** Think again – it could result in harsh-tasting soup *(the raw alcohol taste doesn't cook off in a slow cooker)*.

- **Veggies?** Of course! But toss in fast-cooking ones like peas toward the end of cooking to keep color vibrant and avoid mush.

- **Pasta, rice & grains?** They'll become tender and yummy when slow-cooked. For best results, add and cook as directed in each recipe.

- **Milk? Cheese? Sour cream?** Yes, yes, and yes, but add them at the end of cooking to prevent curdling, which is never a good thing.

Slow-cooking frees you up to do all those things you never seem to have any time for. So grab your cooker and make a batch of happy!

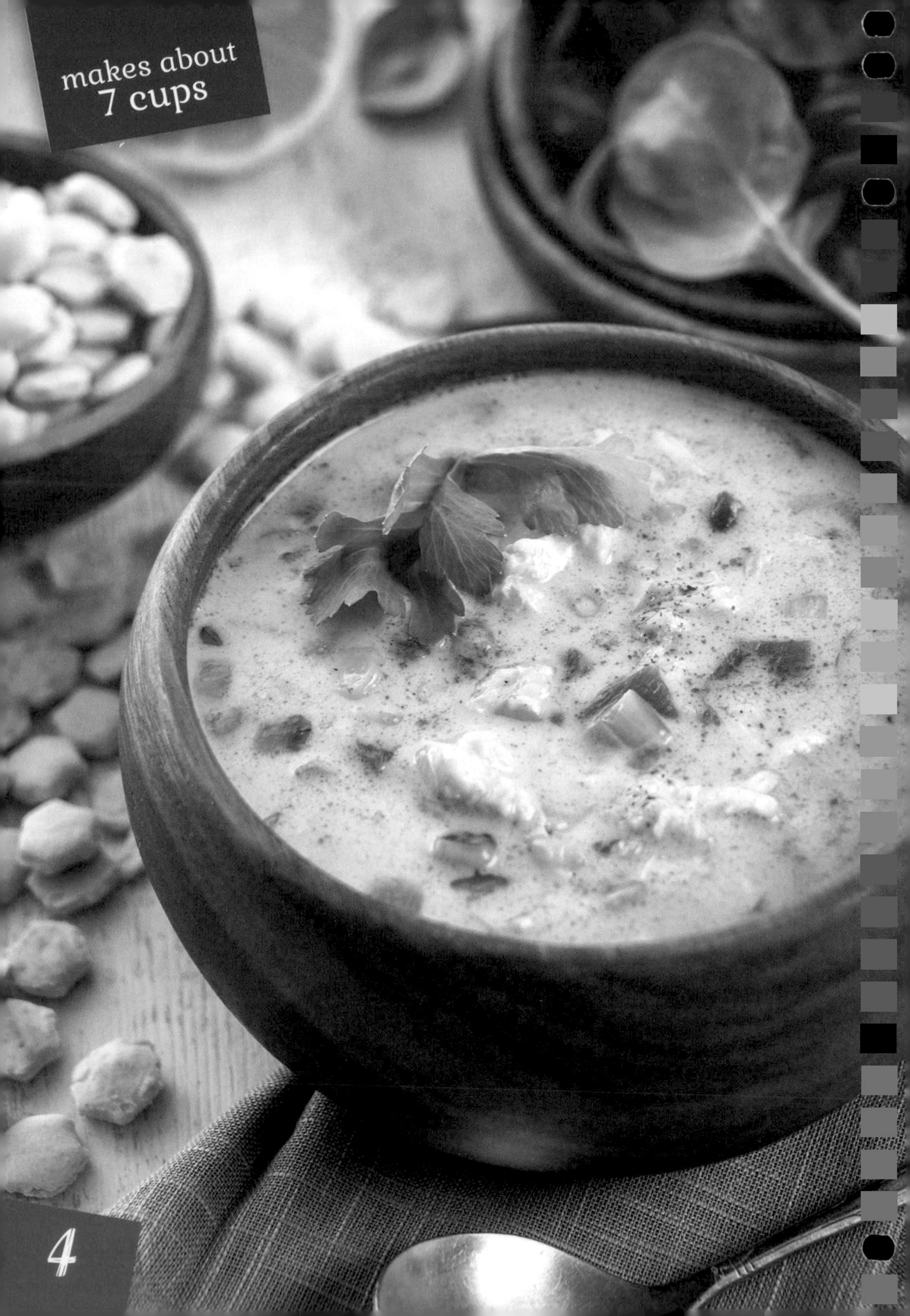
makes about
7 cups

Crab Chowder with Roasted Veggies

1 T. canola oil

1½ C. frozen corn

1 onion, chopped

1 celery rib, chopped

1 (10 oz.) jar roasted red peppers, drained & chopped

1 clove garlic, minced

¼ tsp. each cayenne pepper and ground thyme

2 tsp. Old Bay seasoning

2 (14.5 oz.) cans chicken broth

¼ C. flour

¾ C. heavy cream

4 oz. fontina cheese, cubed

1 (6 oz.) pkg. refrigerated lump crabmeat, flaked

Heat the oil in a big skillet; add the corn, onion, and celery and sauté until lightly browned.

Dump everything from the skillet into a 3-quart slow cooker. Add the roasted peppers, garlic, cayenne pepper, thyme, Old Bay, and broth. Cover and cook on low 6 hours *(high, 3 hours)*.

Combine the flour and cream in a small lidded container; put on the lid, shake it like crazy, and stir slowly into the soup. Cook 30 minutes longer.

Stir in the cheese and crab and let stand until the cheese is melted. Give it a stir and serve it up.

Slow & Easy French Onion

Coat a 6-qt. slow cooker with cooking spray and toss in ¼ C. unsalted butter *(cut up)*, 6 sprigs fresh thyme, 1 bay leaf, and 16 C. *(about 5 lbs.)* sliced sweet onions; sprinkle with 1 T. sugar. Cover and cook on high 8 hours.

Remove and discard the herbs. Stir in 6 C. beef stock, 2 T. red wine vinegar, 1½ tsp. salt, and 1 tsp. black pepper. Cover and cook on high 30 minutes. Preheat the broiler. Spritz cooking spray on both sides of French bread slices *(one slice for each serving of soup)* and broil until toasted on both sides.

Ladle soup into heat-proof bowls set on a rimmed baking sheet; top each with toasted bread and a handful of shredded Irish cheddar cheese. Broil until the cheese melts.

makes about 12 cups

Savory Beef Stew

In a big zippered plastic bag, mix 2 (1 oz.) pkgs. dry onion soup mix and ½ tsp. paprika. Throw in 2 lbs. beef stew meat *(trimmed & cut into bite-size pieces)* and shake to coat.

Toss the coated meat into a 5-qt. slow cooker. Add 5 potatoes *(peeled & diced)*, 3 C. baby carrots *(halved)*, and 1 onion *(chopped)*. Stir together 2 (10 oz.) cans cream of celery soup and 1 C. ketchup and pour into the cooker; season with black pepper. Stir it up, cover, and cook on low for 8 hours *(high, 4 hours)*, until everything is tender.

makes about
8 cups

Creamy Broccoli-Cheese

- ¼ C. butter
- ¼ C. flour
- 3 C. whole milk
- 3 C. chicken broth
- 1 small yellow onion, chopped
- 3 cloves garlic, smashed
- 4 C. fresh broccoli florets

- 2 oz. cream cheese, cubed
- 1 tsp. each salt and black pepper
- ½ tsp. Italian seasoning
- 3 C. shredded cheddar cheese, plus more for serving

Melt the butter in a saucepan over medium heat and whisk in the flour until thick and smooth. Whisk in the milk until fully incorporated. Cook until slightly thickened, whisking often, then remove from the heat.

Pour the broth into a 4-quart slow cooker. Stir in the onion, garlic, broccoli, cream cheese, salt, black pepper, Italian seasoning, and thickened milk. Cover and cook on low 6 hours *(high, 3 hours)*.

Turn off the cooker and stir in 3 cups of cheese; let set until the cheese melts. Top each serving with more cheese.

Cheesy Grilled Steak Sandwiches

Marinate ½ lb. boneless ribeye steak for a couple of hours in a mixture of ½ C. bold & spicy steak sauce, ¼ C. BBQ sauce, and 1½ tsp. minced garlic. Discard the marinade, season the steak with salt, and grill until done to your liking; tent with foil, set aside for 5 minutes, then thinly slice. Cut a tomato into four thick slices, drizzle with olive oil, and season with salt and black pepper; grill until lightly browned on both sides. Grill four slices of potato bread on one side; flip and add some shredded mozzarella and crumbled feta to two slices. When the cheese is melty, remove from the grill. To the cheese, add chopped fresh chives and parsley, grilled tomatoes, and steak slices; top with the remaining toasted bread. Cut in half and share. **Serves 4**

Beefy Chipotle Chili

2 T. butter

1 lb. lean ground beef

¾ C. each diced onion, celery, and green bell pepper

2 cloves garlic, minced

1 (8 oz.) can tomato sauce

2 tomatoes, chopped

2 (15 oz.) cans kidney beans, drained & rinsed

1 (15 oz.) can cannellini beans, drained & rinsed

1½ tsp. chili powder

½ to 1 tsp. chipotle chili powder

1 tsp. salt

¾ tsp. each dried basil, oregano, and parsley

¼ tsp. black pepper

A few dashes of hot sauce

1 (5.5 oz.) can V8 juice

1½ C. beef stock

Cotija or queso fresco cheese, crumbled

Sliced green onions

Melt the butter in a big skillet and add the beef, onion, celery, bell pepper, and garlic. Cook until the meat is no longer pink, crumbling it as it cooks; drain.

Dump everything from the skillet into a 3-quart slow cooker. Stir in the tomato sauce, tomatoes, all the beans, both kinds of chili powder, salt, basil, oregano, parsley, black pepper, hot sauce, V8, and stock. Cover and cook on low for 8 hours *(high, 4 hours)*.

Top each serving with cheese and green onions. .

Canadian Bacon Chowder

In a 3-qt. slow cooker, combine 2 C. diced Yukon gold potatoes, 1 carrot *(diced)*, 1 C. chopped leeks *(white and light green parts)*, ½ tsp. minced garlic, 4 C. chicken broth, ½ C. uncooked medium pearled barley, 1 bay leaf, ¼ tsp. dried thyme *(crushed)*, ¼ tsp. black pepper, 6 oz. diced Canadian bacon, and 4 oz. fresh mushrooms *(diced)*; stir to blend. Cover and cook on low 6 hours *(high, 3 hours)*.

Stir in 1 (5 oz.) can evaporated milk and ¼ C. half & half. Leave the lid off and cook 15 minutes longer or until heated through.

Cabbage Roll Soup

Heat 2 T. olive oil in a skillet over medium-high heat. Add ½ C. each chopped onion and shallots and cook until softened. Add 2 lbs. lean ground beef and 1 tsp. minced garlic and cook until the meat is browned, crumbling it as it cooks; drain.

Dump everything from the skillet into a 7-qt. slow cooker. Sprinkle in 1 tsp. each salt, black pepper, and dried parsley and ½ tsp. each cayenne pepper and dried oregano. Add ½ head cauliflower *(coarsely chopped)*, 1 cabbage *(coarsely chopped)*, 1 (16 oz.) jar marinara sauce, and 5 C. beef broth. Stir until well mixed. Cover and cook on low 6 hours *(high, 3 hours)* or until cabbage is tender.

Sprinkle each serving with shredded Parmesan cheese.

Mexican Rice & Bean Soup

- 1 small onion, diced
- 2 cloves garlic, minced
- ½ tsp. each ground cumin and chili powder
- 1 T. olive oil
- 1 (15.25 oz.) can black beans, drained & rinsed
- 1 (14.5 oz.) can petite diced tomatoes with green chiles *(don't drain)*
- 1 (10 oz.) can petite diced tomatoes with lime and cilantro *(don't drain)*
- 1 (11 oz.) can white corn *(don't drain)*
- ½ C. uncooked long-grain white rice
- 3 C. water
- ¼ tsp. each salt and black pepper
- ¼ C. chopped fresh cilantro
- Juice of 1 lime
- Guacamole and shredded Pepper Jack cheese

In a small skillet, sauté onion, garlic, cumin, and chili powder in hot oil about 5 minutes.

Dump everything from the skillet into a 3-quart slow cooker. Toss in the beans, all the tomatoes, corn, and rice. Add the water and season with salt and black pepper. Stir everything together. Cook on low for 6 hours *(high, 3 hours)* or until the rice is tender.

Turn off the cooker and stir in the cilantro and lime juice. Top each serving with guacamole and cheese.

Mexican Club Sandwiches

Cook 3 bacon strips in a skillet until crisp; set the bacon on paper towels to drain and brush bacon drippings on both sides of 3 (8") flour tortillas. Broil about 1 minute on each side, until just starting to brown, popping air bubbles as they appear. Spread some guacamole on one of the tortillas; top with a handful of shredded lettuce, 4 oz. deli-sliced turkey, and 3 slices Pepper Jack cheese. Add another tortilla; top with more shredded lettuce, the cooked bacon *(crumbled)*, and 4 tomato slices. Mix 2 T. salsa with 1 T. sour cream, spread it evenly over the remaining tortilla, and place it on top with the creamy salsa side down. Cut the stack into four wedges.
Serves 4

makes about 15 cups

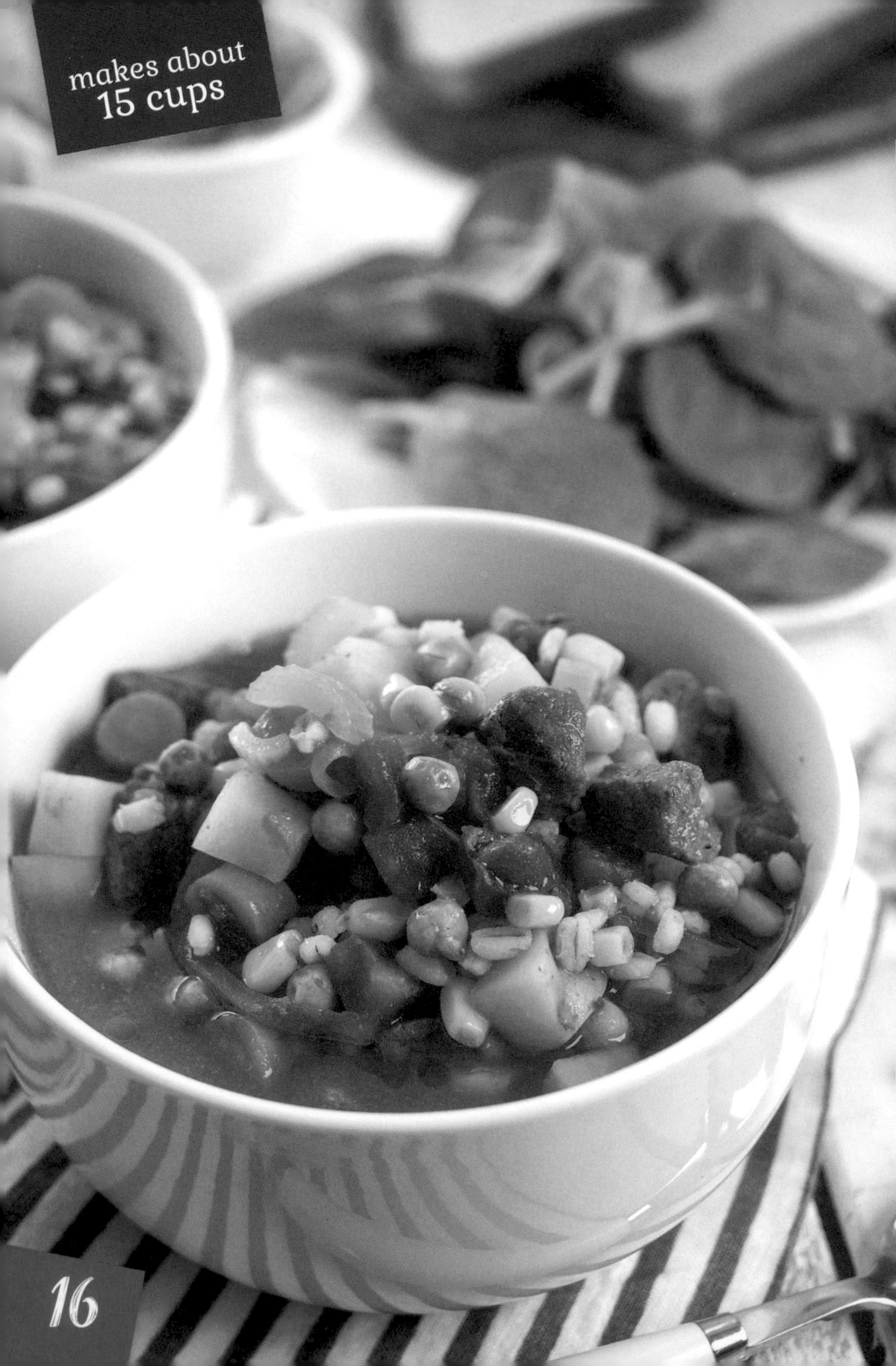

Vegetable Beef & Barley

1 tsp. each seasoned salt, onion powder, and garlic powder

1½ lbs. beef stew meat, trimmed & cut into bite-size pieces

2 T. canola oil

4 C. water

3 Yukon gold potatoes, diced

1 C. each sliced carrots and celery

½ C. chopped onion

1 T. French onion-flavored beef bouillon granules *(such as Wyler's Shakers)*

1 (15.25 oz.) can whole kernel corn, drained

1 (14.5 oz.) can diced tomatoes *(don't drain)*

1 C. tomato juice

¾ C. uncooked medium pearled barley

1½ tsp. salt

1 tsp. black pepper

1 C. frozen peas, thawed

In a big zippered plastic bag, combine the seasoned salt, onion powder, and garlic powder. Shake it up to blend. Toss in the beef pieces and shake until thoroughly coated.

Heat the oil in a big skillet. Add the coated meat and cook until browned on all sides; drain.

Toss the cooked meat into a 5-quart slow cooker and add the water, potatoes, carrots, celery, onion, and bouillon. Cover and cook on low 6 hours *(high, 3 hours)*.

Stir in the corn, tomatoes, tomato juice, barley, salt, and black pepper. Cover and cook on low 2 hours longer or until the barley is tender.

Stir in the peas and serve.

makes about 13 cups

Corn Chowder with a Kick

In a 4-qt. slow cooker, stir together 2 (14.75 oz.) cans cream-style corn, 2 C. frozen sweet corn, 2 (10.5 oz.) cans cream of mushroom soup, 2 (4 oz.) cans chopped green chiles, 2 C. frozen O'Brien hash browns, 2 C. cubed cooked ham, 1 C. frozen chopped onions, 2 T. butter *(sliced)*, 2 T. hot sauce, 2 tsp. dried parsley, 1 tsp. chili powder, and 3 C. milk. Season with salt and black pepper to taste. Cover and cook on low 6 hours *(high, 3 hours)*.

Sprinkle each serving with a handful of crisply cooked bacon *(crumbled)*.

Crockin' Taco Soup

Cook 1 lb. ground pork until done, crumbling it as it cooks; drain and put into a 3-qt. slow cooker. Add 1 (16 oz.) jar salsa, 1 (4 oz.) can diced green chiles, 1 (15 oz.) can black beans *(drained & rinsed)*, 1 C. frozen white corn, 1 diced onion, ½ diced bell pepper *(any color)*, 1 (1 oz.) pkg. taco seasoning mix, 1 tsp. ground cumin, and 3 C. chicken broth. Whisk together 3 T. flour and 1 C. chicken broth until smooth; slowly stir into the cooker. Cook on low 6 hours *(high, 3 hours)*.

Top each serving with sour cream, shredded cheddar cheese, and any of your favorite taco toppings.

makes about
12 cups

Tomato-Basil Soup

3 (15 oz.) cans petite diced tomatoes *(don't drain)*

1 C. each finely chopped celery, onion, and carrots

3 C. chicken broth

½ C. butter

½ C. flour

2 C. half & half

½ C. each shredded Parmesan and Asiago cheeses, plus more for serving

1 tsp. salt

½ tsp. ground oregano

¼ C. chopped fresh basil

Black pepper to taste

In a 4-quart slow cooker, combine the tomatoes, celery, onion, carrots, and broth. Cover and cook on low 6 hours *(high, 3 hours)*.

Melt the butter in a big saucepan over medium heat and then whisk in the flour until thick and smooth. Slowly whisk in the half & half plus 1 to 2 C. of the soup from the cooker; whisk until well blended.

Pour the blended mixture into the cooker, add ½ cup of both cheeses, and stir until melted. Stir in the salt, oregano, basil, and black pepper; cover and cook on low 30 minutes longer.

Blend the soup with an immersion blender until nice and smooth.

Toss a little extra cheese onto each serving.

Pesto Chicken on Ciabatta

Season ¾ lb. chicken breast with Montreal chicken seasoning and broil until done; thinly slice. Cut 4 ciabatta rolls in half; broil until toasted. Mix 2 T. each mayo and sun-dried tomato pesto and spread on cut side of buns. Arrange chicken on bun bottoms, add shredded mozzarella, and broil until cheese melts. Top with sliced roasted red peppers, a slather of guacamole, and fresh basil leaves. Add toasted bun tops. **Makes 4**

Old-Fashioned Beef & Noodle

2 tsp. olive oil

1 lb. beef stew meat, cut into bite-size pieces

1 C. chopped onion

1 C. each sliced fresh mushrooms and carrots

1 red bell pepper, diced

1 (1 oz.) pkg. dry beefy onion soup mix

2 T. tomato paste

1 T. Worcestershire sauce

1 tsp. minced garlic

Salt and black pepper to taste

6 C. water

2½ C. uncooked extra-wide homemade-style egg noodles

Heat oil over medium heat in a skillet and add stew meat and onion, cooking until the meat is brown on all sides; drain.

Toss the meat into a 3-quart slow cooker. Add mushrooms, carrots, bell pepper, dry soup mix, tomato paste, Worcestershire sauce, garlic, salt, and black pepper. Pour in water and give it a quick stir. Cover and cook on low for 6 to 7 hours *(high, 3 to 3½ hours)*, until the vegetables are tender.

Stir in the noodles, cover, and cook 20 to 30 minutes longer or until the noodles are soft.

Bean, Andouille & Spinach

Slice 1 (13.5 oz.) pkg. andouille sausage and brown in a skillet; drain and dump into a 4-qt. slow cooker. Add 2 (15 oz.) cans northern white beans *(drained & rinsed)*, 4 C. chicken broth, 2 C. salsa, 1 C. frozen carrots, ½ C. diced red onion, ½ C. sliced celery, ½ C. chopped parsley, and 2 tsp. each Creole seasoning, garlic powder, onion powder, and black pepper. Cover and cook on low 8 hours *(high, 4 hours)*.

Stir in 3 C. baby spinach and cook 15 minutes longer or until the spinach is just wilted.

makes about
14 cups

Turkey & Wild Rice

In a 5-qt. slow cooker, mix 1 lb. diced cooked turkey, 1 C. uncooked wild rice, 1 C. sliced mushrooms, 1 (10 oz.) pkg. frozen mixed vegetables *(carrots, onions, celery & peppers)*, 4 C. chicken stock, 4 C. water, 2 T. chicken bouillon powder, 2 T. dry chicken soup base, and some salt and black pepper. Cover and cook on low 6 hours *(high, 3 hours)*.

Melt ¼ C. butter in a saucepan over medium heat; whisk in ½ C. flour until smooth. Stir in 1 C. each heavy cream and half & half, 2 C. chicken stock, 1 T. dried parsley, and ½ tsp. each salt and black pepper and cook until thickened, whisking constantly; add to the cooker along with 1 C. frozen *mixed vegetables (corn, peas, & green beans)*. Cook uncovered on low for 30 minutes, until thickened.

Cheesy Potato Soup

1 (32 oz.) pkg. frozen diced
   hash browns

½ C. frozen chopped onion

1 celery rib, chopped

4 C. chicken broth

1 C. water

3 T. flour

1 C. milk

½ tsp. black pepper

1 C. each cubed American
   and cheddar cheeses

Shredded cheddar cheese

Cooked & crumbled bacon

Chopped chives

Put the hash browns, onion, celery, broth, and water into a 3-quart slow cooker. Cover and cook on low 8 hours *(high, 4 hours)*.

Whisk together the flour, milk, and black pepper until smooth; stir into the soup. Cover and cook on high 30 minutes longer, until the soup thickens. Stir in both cubed cheeses, cover, and let stand until melted.

Top each serving with shredded cheese, bacon, and chives.

Buffalo Chicken Roll-Ups

Preheat the oven to 375°. Mix 1 large chicken breast half *(cooked & shredded)* with ½ (8 oz.) pkg. cream cheese *(softened)*, ⅓ C. buffalo wing sauce, 2 T. blue cheese dressing, and 3 green onions *(thinly sliced)*. Unroll 1 (8 oz.) tube refrigerated crescent dough sheet on parchment paper and spread evenly with the chicken mixture. Starting with one long side, roll up and pinch the edges to seal in the filling. Use unflavored dental floss to cut the roll into 1" slices; set the slices on an ungreased cookie sheet. Bake 15 to 18 minutes or until nicely browned. Serve with wing sauce or blue cheese dressing for dipping if you'd like. ***Makes about 12***

Beef Fajita Soup

1½ lbs. boneless beef sirloin steak, trimmed

1 tsp. each ground cumin, paprika, and black pepper

Sea salt

Chili powder

1 tsp. olive oil

1 each yellow, orange, and green bell pepper, chopped

½ jalapeño pepper, sliced, plus more for serving *(optional)*

1 C. fresh salsa

2 tsp. minced garlic

Juice of 1 lime

4 C. beef broth

Diced avocado

Put the steak in the freezer for 30 minutes to make it easier to slice, then cut it into thin, bite-size pieces. Mix cumin, paprika, black pepper, 1 teaspoon sea salt, and ½ to 1 tablespoon chili powder in a zippered plastic bag; toss in the meat and shake to coat.

In a skillet, cook the meat in hot oil until browned and then toss into a 3-quart slow cooker. Add the bell peppers, ½ jalapeño, salsa, garlic, lime juice, and broth; stir. Cover and cook on low 6 hours *(high, 3 hours)*, until everything is tender.

Top each serving with avocado and more jalapeño slices.

To make tortilla chips, cut 8 corn tortillas into six wedges each. Heat 2 C. canola oil to 365° in a big skillet. Fry the wedges a few at a time in the hot oil until crisp; transfer to paper towels and immediately brush with lime juice and sprinkle with a little sea salt and chili powder. Serve the chips with the soup.

Hearty Ham & Bean

Toss 1 large yellow onion *(chopped)* and 2 celery ribs *(chopped)* into a 3-qt. slow cooker. Add 1 meaty ham bone or several ham hocks, 1 (1 lb.) pkg. dry 15-bean mix *(picked over & rinsed)*, 2 bay leaves, and 1 T. minced garlic; season with black pepper. Pour in 6 to 8 C. vegetable broth *(enough to cover the vegetables)*. Cover and cook on low for 8 hours, until everything is tender.

Remove and discard the bay leaves; remove the meat, discarding the fat and bones. Shred or chop the meat and return to the cooker, stirring to combine.

Easy Minestrone

In a skillet, cook 1 lb. ground pork sausage, crumbling it as it cooks; drain.

Toss the meat into a 4-qt. slow cooker. Stir in 1 tsp. garlic powder, 2 (19 oz.) cans ready-to-eat minestrone soup, 2 (15 oz.) cans ranch-style beans, 1 (15.25 oz.) can whole kernel corn *(drained)*, and 1 (28 oz.) can crushed tomatoes with basil. Cover and cook on low 5 hours *(high, 2½ hours)*.

Top each serving with sour cream and your favorite shredded cheese.

makes about
7 cups

Creamy Cauliflower-Parsnip

1 head cauliflower, cut into florets

3 large parsnips, peeled & sliced

2 tsp. minced garlic

1 T. chicken bouillon powder

3 C. water

2 tsp. coconut oil

1 lg. onion, thinly sliced

Salt

1 Granny Smith apple

½ C. coconut milk or heavy cream

Black pepper to taste

In a 3-quart slow cooker, layer the cauliflower, parsnips, and garlic. Mix bouillon powder with water and pour into the cooker, adding more water if needed so veggies are just covered. Cover and cook on low for 7 hours *(high, 3½ hours).*

About 30 minutes before the end of cooking time, heat the oil over medium heat in a big skillet. Add the onion and a pinch of salt and cook until just beginning to brown. Dice the apple and toss it into the skillet with the onion; cook for 30 minutes or until onion is golden brown, stirring occasionally.

At the end of cooking time, stir coconut milk into the cooker and season with salt and black pepper to taste. Puree with an immersion blender until the desired consistency is reached.

Ladle into bowls and top each with some of the onion mixture.

Loaded Italian Grilled Cheese

*Sauté 1 (13 oz.) pkg. cooked Italian herb sausage (sliced) along with 1 each red and orange bell pepper and 1 small yellow onion (sliced) in hot oil until vegetables have softened. Melt 2 T. butter in a separate skillet on medium-low heat and add four slices ciabatta bread; top with dried parsley and shredded enchilado, gouda, and Munster cheeses. Add some of the sausage mixture, even more cheese, and another bread slice to each. Brown both sides. Cut in half and share. **Serves 8***

Turkey Pot Pie in a Bowl

1 T. olive oil

2 lbs. turkey meat, cut into bite-size pieces

1½ tsp. each salt and black pepper

1 small yellow onion, diced

1 tsp. minced garlic

3 celery ribs, diced

1 (16 oz.) bag frozen peas & carrots

1½ C. diced Yukon gold potatoes

2 fresh thyme sprigs

6 C. chicken stock

¾ C. half & half

¼ C. flour

Heat the oil in a big skillet and add the meat. Cook until golden brown; drain.

Toss the meat into a 3-quart slow cooker and season with salt and black pepper. Add the onion, garlic, celery, peas and carrots, potatoes, thyme, and stock.

In a small lidded container, combine the half & half and flour; put on the lid, shake well, and stir slowly into soup. Cover and cook on low 6 hours *(high, 3 hours)* or until the potatoes are tender.

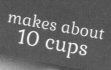

![Chicken Tortilla Soup photo]

makes about
8 cups

Chicken Tortilla Soup

In a 3-qt. slow cooker, stir together 1 (11 oz.) can condensed fiesta nacho cheese soup, 1 (10.7 oz.) can cream of chicken soup, 2 (10 oz.) cans chunk chicken *(drained)*, 1¼ C. enchilada sauce, and 1 (4.25 oz.) can chopped green chiles. Cook on low 3 hours.

Stir in 2⅔ C. milk and cook 30 minutes longer, until hot.

Top each serving with shredded cheddar cheese, sour cream, tortilla strips, and sliced green onions.

Almost Lasagna Soup

In a 3-qt. slow cooker, mix 1 (28 oz.) can diced tomatoes and 1 (6 oz.) can tomato paste. Stir in 3 C. vegetable stock, 1 (12 oz.) pkg. frozen veggie crumbles *(such as Morning Star Farms Grillers)*, 1 T. minced garlic, 1 T. each dried parsley and dried basil, ½ C. chopped onion, 2 (5.5 oz.) cans V8 juice, and 1 tsp. each salt and black pepper. Cover and cook on low 8 hours *(high, 4 hours)*.

Add 1 C. water and 2 C. uncooked mafalda pasta *(mini lasagna noodles);* stir to combine. Cover and cook 30 minutes longer, until pasta is tender. Top each serving with shredded mozzarella and shredded Parmesan cheeses.

Granny Smith Squash Soup

1 large onion, cut into chunks

1 T. olive oil

8 C. peeled, seeded & cubed butternut squash *(about 2 medium)*

2 T. brown sugar

¾ tsp. each salt and cinnamon

⅛ tsp. white pepper

3 C. chicken broth

2 large Granny Smith apples, divided

¾ C. milk

1 (6 oz.) container plain Greek yogurt, plus more for serving

Cooked & crumbled bacon

38

In a skillet, cook onion in oil until softened. Transfer to a 6-quart slow cooker and add squash, brown sugar, salt, cinnamon, white pepper, and broth; peel and chop one of the apples and add it to the cooker. Give it a good stir, cover, and cook on low 6 hours *(high, 3 hours)*, until squash is tender.

Use an immersion blender to blend the soup until silky smooth. Stir in the milk and 6 ounces of yogurt.

Cut the remaining apple into matchsticks. Top each serving of soup with more yogurt, some bacon, and the apple matchsticks.

Turkey-Brie 'Wiches

Preheat the oven to 375°. Stir together ¼ C. each mayo and Sriracha mayo and ½ tsp. chili powder; set aside. Set 4 slices ciabatta bread on a baking sheet; on two of the bread slices, layer oven-roasted deli turkey slices, fresh peach slices, and some brie cheese *(the other two bread slices will toast without toppings)*. Bake 10 to 15 minutes, until the cheese melts. Put some arugula on the melty cheese, spread the set-aside mayo mixture over the plain toasted bread, and put sandwiches together. Cut in half and share. *(For a sweet version of this sandwich, omit the mayo mixture and arugula, and sprinkle brown sugar over the cheese before baking).* **Serves 4**

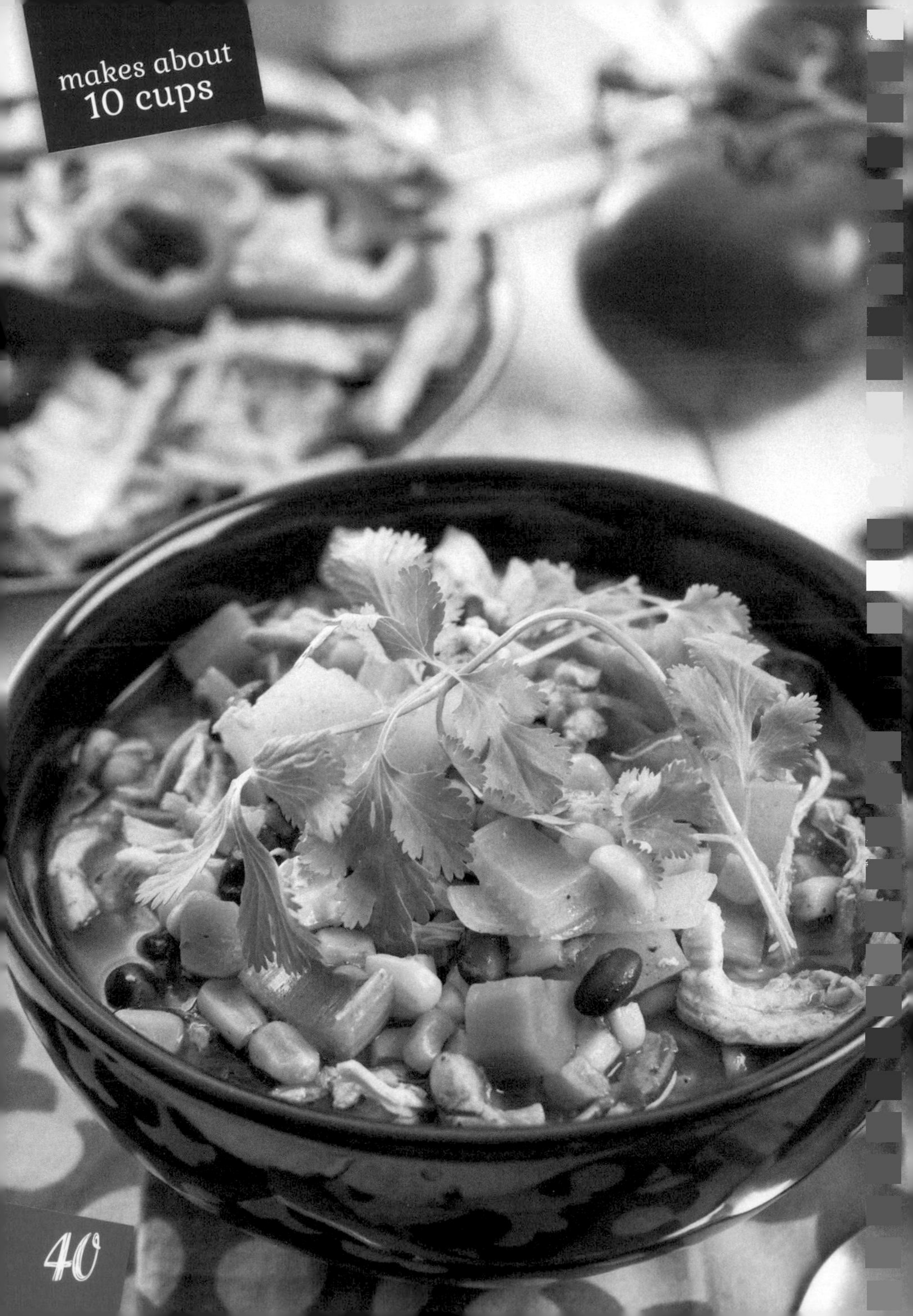
makes about
10 cups

Southwest Chicken Stew

2 baking potatoes, peeled & cut into chunks *(3 to 4 C.)*

1 (12 oz.) pkg. frozen Southwest vegetable blend

2 each celery ribs and carrots, sliced

1 onion, sliced

1 tsp. minced garlic

1 C. spicy salsa

1½ tsp. ground cumin

1 tsp. chili powder

½ tsp. black pepper

A few dashes of hot sauce

2 boneless, skinless chicken breasts

2 boneless, skinless chicken thighs

3½ C. chicken broth

1 tsp. salt

In a 4-quart slow cooker, stir together the potatoes, southwest vegetables, celery, carrots, onion, garlic, salsa, cumin, chili powder, black pepper, and hot sauce. Lay all the chicken pieces on top and pour in the broth. Cover and cook on high 4 hours.

Remove and shred the meat, sprinkle generously with salt, and return to the cooker. Stir and serve.

Adjust the seasonings in this recipe to fit your taste. By adding frozen Southwest vegetables, you get instant added flavor. Zip and zing included.

Shortcut Meatball Stew

Toss 1 (14 oz.) bag frozen homestyle meatballs into a
4-qt. slow cooker. Add 1 (15 oz.) can crushed tomatoes
(don't drain), 1 (8 oz.) can tomato sauce, 2 (14.5 oz.) cans
beef broth, 2 C. water, ½ C. each frozen carrots, frozen
pearl onions, frozen corn, shelled edamame, and bell
pepper *(any color)*. Cover and cook on low for 5 hours
(high, 2½ hours) or until the vegetables are tender.

Stir 1½ C. small shell pasta into the cooker and season
with salt, black pepper, garlic powder, and cayenne pepper
to taste. Stir in ½ C. chopped fresh parsley and cook
45 minutes longer, until the pasta is cooked to perfection.

Buffalo Chicken Noodle

In a 3-qt. slow cooker, mix 2 C. shredded rotisserie chicken, 4 each celery ribs and carrots *(chopped)*, 1 small yellow onion *(chopped)*, 2 tsp. minced garlic, 1½ T. dry ranch dressing mix, ½ C. buffalo wing sauce, and 6 C. chicken stock. Cover and cook on low 6 hours *(high, 3 hours)*, until veggies are tender.

Whisk together 2 T. cornstarch and 2 T. cold water until smooth, and stir into the cooker. Season soup with salt and black pepper and add more wing sauce if you like it spicier. Add 2½ C. uncooked wide egg noodles and ¼ C. chopped fresh parsley. Cook for 10 minutes or until the noodles have softened.

Top each serving with blue cheese crumbles.

Chunky Couscous Soup

1 T. butter

1 each onion and green
bell pepper, finely
chopped

1 C. finely chopped carrots

2 (15 oz.) cans kidney
beans (drained & rinsed)

1 C. uncooked couscous

1 (14.5 oz.) can stewed
tomatoes (don't drain)

1 C. marinara sauce

1 tsp. each salt and
dried basil

¼ tsp. black pepper

½ tsp. cayenne pepper

4 C. vegetable stock

Melt the butter in a big skillet. Add onion, bell pepper, and carrots. Cook about 10 minutes.

Transfer everything from the skillet to a 3-quart slow cooker. Stir in kidney beans, couscous, tomatoes, marinara sauce, salt, basil, black pepper, cayenne pepper, and stock. Cover and cook on low 3 hours, until the vegetables are tender.

Turn off the cooker. Stir, cover, and let stand 30 minutes before serving to give the soup a chance to thicken up a bit.

Couscous [KOOS-koos]: These little pearls of versatility can be eaten hot or cold, stirred into a salad or tucked into a sandwich, quick-cooked or tossed into a slow cooker to leisurely morph into the yummiest of comfort food. Enjoy!

Veggie & Hummas Flats

Toss 1⅓ C. halved cherry tomatoes into a bowl with a cucumber (chopped), and a small red onion (diced); drizzle with a little olive oil and sprinkle with salt and black pepper to taste. Stir to blend. Spread each of four flatbreads with a good amount of your favorite hummus. Divide the vegetable mixture evenly among the flatbreads and toss on a handful of feta cheese crumbles. Add sliced black or green olives if you'd like. Fold and eat.

45

Spicy Italian Sausage

1 lb. ground spicy Italian sausage

½ lb. hickory-smoked bacon, chopped

4 C. water

4 C. chicken broth

1 lg. sweet potato, peeled & cubed

2 cloves garlic, crushed

1 small onion, chopped

2 C. chopped fresh kale

1 C. heavy cream

Salt and black pepper to taste

Shredded Romano cheese

In a hot skillet, brown the sausage and bacon, breaking up the sausage as it cooks; drain.

Dump the meat into a 4-quart slow cooker. Add the water, broth, sweet potato, garlic, and onion. Cover and cook on low 6 hours *(high, 3 hours)*, until veggies are tender.

Add the kale and cream and season with salt and black pepper. Leave the lid off and cook 15 minutes longer or until heated through and kale is wilted.

Top each serving with cheese.

makes about
8 cups

Thai Pork Stew

In a 3-qt. slow cooker, mix 2 lbs. boneless pork loin *(cut into bite-size pieces)*, 2 C. julienned red bell peppers, 2 C. beef stock, ¼ C. teriyaki sauce, 2 T. rice wine vinegar, 1 tsp. red pepper flakes, 2 cloves garlic *(minced)*, and ½ tsp. salt. Cover and cook on low 7 hours *(high, 3½ hours)*.

Stir in 1 C. uncooked instant rice and 1 (14 oz.) can coconut milk; cook on low for 20 minutes, until rice is tender. Add 1 (7 oz.) jar baby corn *(drained)* and ¼ C. creamy peanut butter; stir until peanut butter is melted.

Top each serving with green onions and peanuts.

Meatballs & Tortellini

In a microwave-safe bowl, mix 2 tsp. each dried basil and dried oregano, 1 onion *(finely chopped)*, 1 C. shredded carrots, 1 T. tomato paste, 2 cloves garlic *(minced)*, and 2 T. olive oil. Microwave on high 5 minutes, stirring every 1½ minutes. Transfer the mixture to a 6-qt. slow cooker. Add 1 red bell pepper *(diced)*, 1 (26 oz.) pkg. frozen Italian meatballs, 1 (14.5 oz.) can petite diced tomatoes *(don't drain)*, 1 (15 oz.) can tomato sauce, 1 (19 oz.) pkg. frozen cheese tortellini, 5 tsp. beef bouillon granules, and 5 C. water. Cover and cook on low 6 hours *(high, 3 hours)*.

Stir in 1 zucchini *(diced)* and season with salt and black pepper. Cook 20 minutes longer. Top each serving with shredded mozzarella cheese.

Taste of Tuscany Chicken Soup

1 C. chopped onion

2 T. tomato paste

1 tsp. each salt and black pepper

1 (15 oz.) can cannellini beans, drained & rinsed

1 (14 oz.) can chicken broth

½ (10 oz.) jar roasted red peppers, drained & chopped

1 lb. boneless, skinless chicken thighs, diced

3 cloves garlic, finely chopped

½ tsp. dried rosemary, crushed

1 (6 oz.) pkg. fresh baby spinach

Shredded Parmesan cheese

Toss the onion, tomato paste, salt, black pepper, beans, broth, roasted peppers, chicken, garlic, and rosemary into a 3-quart slow cooker. Cover and cook on high 1 hour.

Reduce the heat to low and cook 3 hours longer.

Stir in the spinach, cover, and cook about 10 minutes, just until the spinach wilts.

Top each serving with cheese.

Also known as white Italian kidney beans, it is said that cannellini beans can provide hours of energy, help stave off cravings, AND control mood swings. Need we say more?

Veg-Out Sandwiches

Thinly slice a carrot, bell pepper (any color), cucumber, tomato, and avocado. Spread a thick layer of purchased spinach dip onto four slices of your favorite bread. Pile the veggies on two of the slices and add a nice layer of baby spinach and a handful of alfalfa sprouts. Top with the remaining bread slices; cut and share.
Serves 4

Summer Pesto Soup

5 C. diced Yukon gold potatoes

1½ C. halved baby carrots

1 C. diced leeks *(white and light green parts)*

2 C. trimmed & sliced fresh green beans

2 yellow or red tomatoes, diced

1 T. each chopped fresh basil and oregano

8 C. water

2 zucchini, cut in half lengthwise & sliced

1 C. frozen lima beans

1 (15.25 oz.) can whole kernel corn, drained

⅔ C. uncooked orzo

⅓ C. prepared basil pesto

Salt and black pepper to taste

Shredded Parmesan cheese

Put the potatoes, carrots, leeks, green beans, tomatoes, basil, oregano, and water into a 5-quart slow cooker. Cover and cook on high 4 hours, until the potatoes are tender.

Add the zucchini, lima beans, corn, and orzo. Cover and cook 30 minutes longer or until everything is tender. Stir in the pesto, and season with plenty of salt and black pepper.

Top each serving with some cheese.

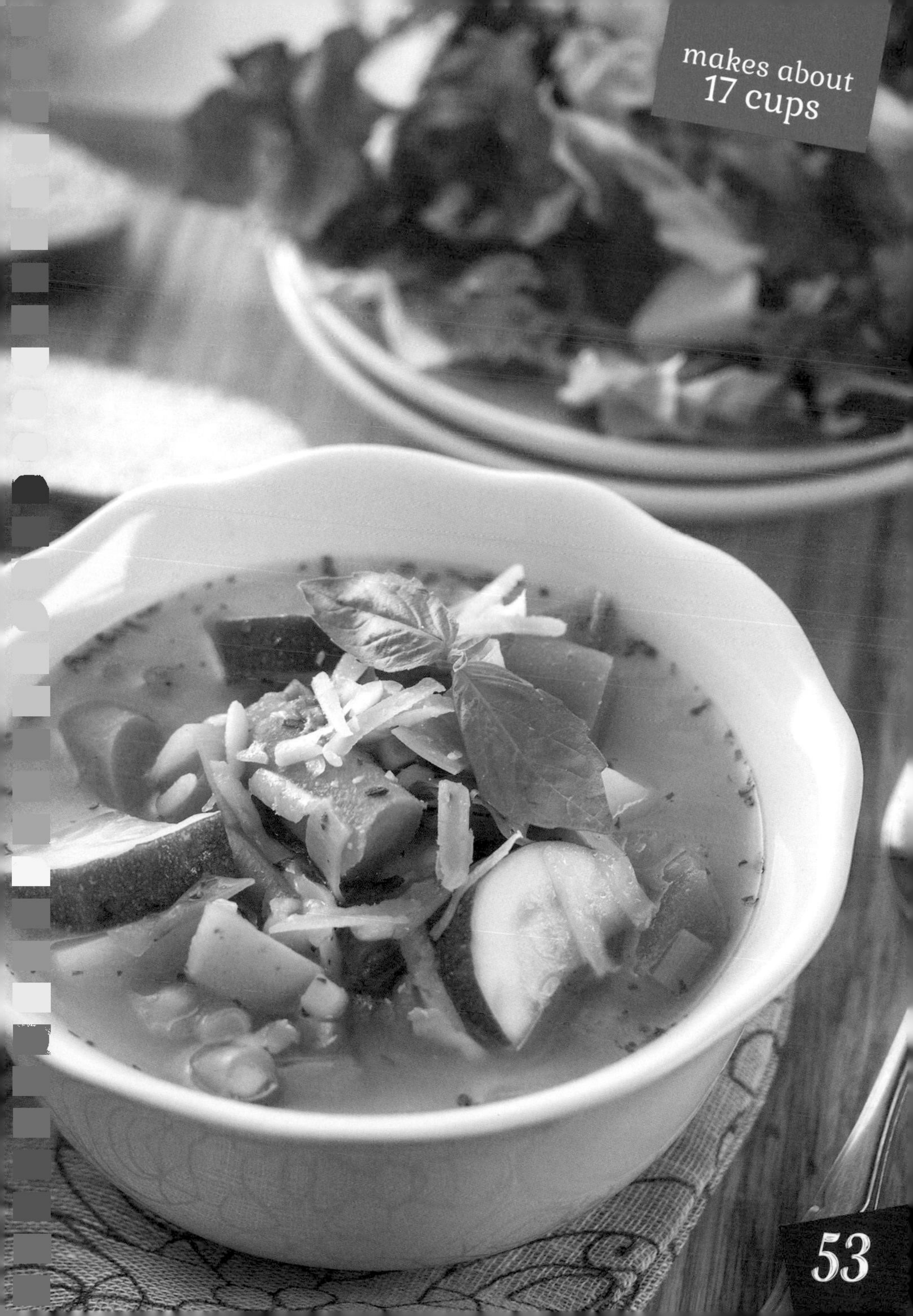

makes about
17 cups

Eastern Clam Chowder

In a 3-qt. slow cooker, combine 1 (6.5 oz.) can chopped clams *(don't drain)*, 1 (10 oz.) can whole baby clams *(don't drain)*, ¼ lb. cooked bacon *(crumbled)*, 1 small white onion *(chopped)*, 4 small white potatoes *(peeled & diced)*, 1¾ tsp. salt, ⅛ tsp. black pepper, and 1½ C. water. Cover and cook on high 3 hours.

Whisk together 1 C. half & half and 2 T. cornstarch until well blended, then stir into the cooker and cook 1 hour longer.

Stir in 1 C. half & half and let stand until heated through.

Split Pea & Smoked Turkey

Use kitchen string to tie together about 10 fresh parsley stems and 4 fresh thyme sprigs; toss them into a big oval slow cooker. Stir in 1 lb. dry green split peas *(picked over & rinsed)*, 1 large leek *(white and light green parts halved lengthwise & thinly sliced)*, 2 each celery ribs and carrots *(chopped)*, 1 tsp. salt, and ½ tsp. black pepper. Add 1 big smoked turkey leg and 7 C. water. Cover and cook on low for 6 to 8 hours, until peas are tender.

Remove and discard the herb bundle. Remove the turkey leg; discard the skin and bones and shred the meat. Whisk the soup to break up some of the peas, stir in ½ C. chopped fresh parsley and the shredded meat, and season with more salt and black pepper.

makes about
14 cups

Hot & Sour Soup

1 (8 oz.) pkg. sliced fresh button or shiitake mushrooms

½ (12 oz.) pkg. broccoli slaw mix

1 (8 oz.) can sliced bamboo shoots, drained & rinsed

1 (12 oz.) pkg. extra-firm water-packed tofu

4⅓ C. water, divided

4 C. vegetable stock

½ C. soy sauce or more to taste

1½ T. Sriracha hot sauce

1 T. ground ginger

3 T. cornstarch

1 T. toasted sesame oil

1 (9 oz.) pkg. frozen sugar snap peas

1 (8 oz.) pkg. rice noodles

1 tsp. ground white pepper

¼ C. each apple cider vinegar and red wine vinegar

Sliced green onions

Sliced jalapeño peppers

Dump the mushrooms in an even layer in a 4-quart slow cooker. Top with the broccoli slaw and bamboo shoots.

Drain and dice the tofu and toss into the cooker. Add 4 cups water, the stock, soy sauce, hot sauce, and ginger and stir until well blended. Cover and cook on low 8 hours (high, 4 hours).

Whisk together the cornstarch, oil, and the remaining ⅓ cup water until lump-free. Slowly stir the mixture into the cooker, cover, and cook for 20 minutes.

Stir in the snap peas and noodles; cover and cook 10 minutes longer, then stir in the white pepper and both vinegars. Taste and adjust seasonings if necessary.

Top each serving with green onions and jalapeños.

Teriyaki Pork Wraps

Trim 1 lb. tenderized boneless pork loin chops, cut into ½"-thick slices, and brown in 1 T. hot canola oil until cooked through. Stir in ½ C. teriyaki sauce, 3 cloves garlic (minced), and 1 tsp. onion powder; cook 3 minutes, stirring often. Divide the mixture off-center among 4 (8") flour tortillas (warmed); top with shredded Romaine lettuce, mandarin orange slices, and french-fried onions. Fold, cut in half, and share.
Serves 8

makes about 12 cups

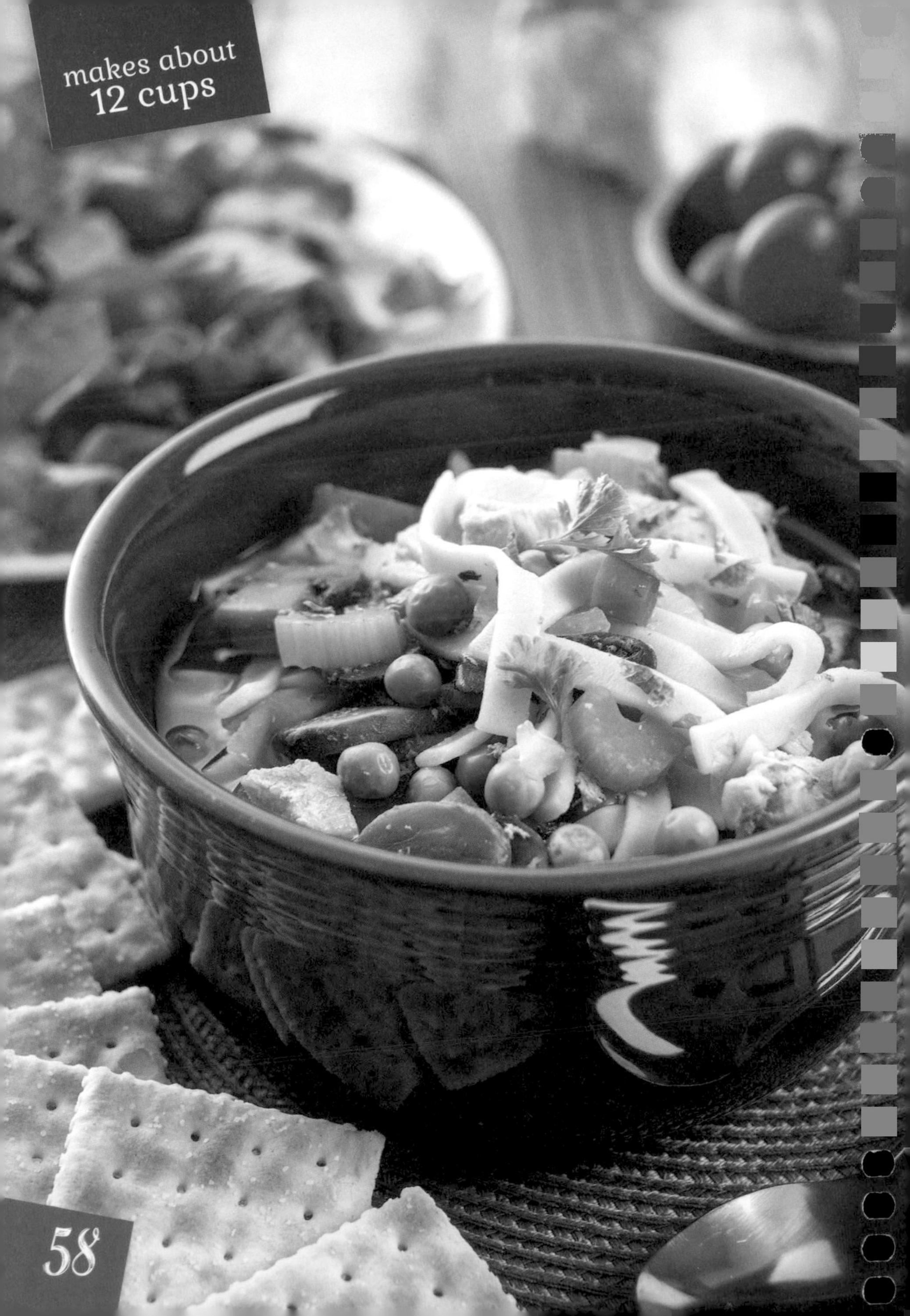

Classic Chicken Noodle

1 onion, sliced

2 each carrots and celery ribs, sliced

4 oz. fresh mushrooms, sliced

1 lb. boneless, skinless chicken breast, cut into bite-size pieces

2 tsp. salt

½ tsp. black pepper

¼ tsp. dried thyme

1 T. dried parsley

5 C. water

2 chicken bouillon cubes

3 C. uncooked thin egg noodles

1 C. frozen peas, thawed

Dump the onion, carrots, celery, mushrooms, and chicken into a 4-quart slow cooker. Sprinkle with the salt, black pepper, thyme, and parsley. Pour the water over the top and toss in the bouillon cubes. Cover and cook on low 8 hours *(high, 4 hours)*.

Stir in the noodles, cover, and cook on high 45 minutes longer or until noodles are tender.

Stir in the peas and serve.

Nothing says lovin' like a bowlful of homemade chicken noodle soup.

makes about
16 cups

Loaded Vegetable Soup

Grab a 5-quart slow cooker and toss in 1 onion *(diced)*,
1 (16 oz.) pkg. frozen mixed vegetables, 1 (15 oz.) can lima
beans *(drained & rinsed)*, 2 C. frozen sweet corn, 1 (16 oz.)
pkg. frozen carrots, 2 (28 oz.) cans petite diced tomatoes
(don't drain), and 2 C. frozen okra. Stir in 2 C. water and
2 to 3 tsp. salt-free seasoning *(such as Mrs. Dash Table
Blend)*. Cover and cook on low 4 hours.

makes about 10 cups

Bacon Cheeseburger Bowls

Brown 1 lb. ground beef with 1 C. diced onion, breaking up the meat as it cooks; drain and dump into a 3-qt. slow cooker. Stir in 1 (14.5 oz.) can diced tomatoes *(don't drain)*, 5 bacon strips *(cooked & crumbled)*, ½ C. chopped celery, 1 C. shredded carrots, 2 C. peeled & diced potatoes, 1 (8 oz.) pkg. cream cheese *(diced)*, 4 C. chicken broth, 2 tsp. minced garlic, 1 tsp. salt, ½ tsp. black pepper, and 1½ tsp. seasoned salt. Cover and cook on low 8 hours *(high, 4 hours)*, until veggies are tender.

Whisk together ¼ C. flour and 1 C. milk until smooth; slowly stir into the cooker. Stir in 2 C. shredded sharp cheddar cheese. Cook uncovered for 10 minutes, until the cheese melts. Top each serving with more cheese and chopped dill pickles.

Start with Homemade

These recipes are guidelines to get you started – you can use any vegetables, herbs, and seasonings that you like.

Vegetable Stock

Chopped fresh vegetables
(any combo)

Salt to taste

Water

5 or 6 sprigs fresh thyme

1 small bunch fresh parsley

A few black peppercorns

2 bay leaves

Fill a big slow cooker about ⅔ full with vegetables, sprinkle with salt, and add enough water to cover. Toss in thyme, parsley, peppercorns, and bay leaves. Cover and cook on high 5 hours. Strain through cheesecloth or a fine mesh strainer into a big bowl; discard solids and strain again. Use the liquid in place of canned vegetable stock. Store in mason jars or freezer containers. Keeps well in the fridge for a few days or in the freezer for a few months.